SECRETS TO DEVELOP AUTHENTIC RELATIONSHIPS

PRACTICAL STRATEGIES FOR CREATING LASTING CONNECTIONS

DR. JAGADEESH PILLAI

Made with ♥ on the Notion Press Platform
www.notionpress.com

|| Dedicated to all wisdom seekers around the world ||

ᑭᑭᑭ

Contents

Contents

Prayer

"Om Bhadram Karnebhih Shrunuyaama DevaahBhadram Pashyemaakshabhiryajatraah SthirairangaistushtuvaamsastanoobhihVyashema Devahitam YadaayuhSwasti Na Indro VridhashravaahSwasti Nah Pooshaa VishwavedaahSwasti Nastaarkshyo ArishtanemihSwasti No Brihaspatir DadhaatuOm Shantih, Shantih, Shantih"

The literal meaning of this mantra is: OM. O Gods! Let us hear auspicious words from our ears. O reverent Gods! Let us behold propitious visions from our eyes, let our organs and body be stable, healthy, and strong. Let us do that which is pleasing to the gods in the life span allotted to us. May Indra, inscribed in the scriptures, bring us fortune! May Pushan, the knower of the world, grant us prosperity! May Trakshya, who vanquishes enemies, bestow us with blessings! May Brihaspati bring us success!
OM Peace, Peace, Peace.

About The Author

Dr. Jagadeesh Pillai is a renowned Guinness World Record holder, writer, and researcher hailing from Varanasi, also known as the abode of Lord Shiva. With a Ph.D. in Vedic Science and a range of creative ideas and achievements, he is a true polymath. He is the author of more than 100 books including Research Publications. Although his roots can be traced back to Kerala, the people of Varanasi hold him in high regard and affectionately consider him one of their own.

In 1998, Dr. Pillai was offered a job at Banaras Hindu University, but he left the position after only two months to pursue greater goals in life. He believed that in order to study Indian scriptures and engage in other creative endeavours, he needed to retire from the daily grind of working solely for money at a young age.

He started an export business from scratch, using the knowledge he had gained from a previous job in the industry. His intelligence and unique approach to business led to great success in a short period of time, earning him more in just a decade and a half than he would have in a lifetime working in a government job. Upon the passing of Dr. APJ Abdul Kalam, Dr. Pillai decided to leave the business and dedicate himself to reading, studying, researching, and experimenting.

During his tenure in the export business, Dr. Pillai traveled to over 16 countries, gaining valuable insight and experiencing the world and life in detail.

Dr. Pillai has achieved four Guinness World Records in the following subjects:

"Script to Screen" - In this record, Dr. Pillai produced and directed an animation film within the shortest time possible, breaking the previous record set by Canadians. He has also received numerous national and international awards and recognitions for this achievement.

Longest Line of Postcards - For this record, Dr. Pillai created a line of 16,300 postcards on the occasion of the 163rd anniversary of Indian Postal Day. The event also included a questionnaire about the Indian flag.

Largest Poster Awareness Campaign - Dr. Pillai designed an awareness campaign on the subject of "Beti Bachao - Beti Padhao" (Save the Girl Child - Educate the Girl Child) to achieve this record.

Largest Envelope - In tribute to the Indian Prime Minister's "Make in India" initiative, Dr. Pillai created a 4000 square meter envelope using waste paper to achieve this record.

Attempted - **70000 Candles on a 210 kg Cake** - To celebrate the 70th Indian Independence Day, Dr. Pillai attempted to light 70,000 candles on a 210 kg cake, which was recorded in World Records India.

Attempted - **Documentary on Dhamek Stupa of Sarnath in 17 Languages** - Dr. Pillai attempted to create a documentary on the Dhamek Stupa of Sarnath, dubbing it in 17 different languages. The result of this attempt is currently awaiting confirmation from the Guinness World Records.

Dr. Pillai is skilled in teaching the Bhagavad Gita, a Hindu scripture, and is popular among young people. He has helped many young people improve their lives through his motivational teachings.

In addition to teaching, he has composed and sung numerous Sanskrit Bhajans and patriotic songs.

He has also written and directed several short films and documentaries for awareness campaigns, and has volunteered with the police in both UP and Kerala to spread awareness about various issues through videos and photography.

Incredibly, he has produced and directed over 100 documentaries about the city of Varanasi, all on his own.

He has also helped and guided more than 25 boys and girls to achieve world records through creative and innovative methods. He is a multifaceted person who uses his intellect and the blessings given to him by God to excel in various areas. He is both a teacher and a student, always learning and teaching, and is able to master any subject he comes across.

He is a selfless social activist and motivational speaker who has overcome struggles and failures to become a successful and enthusiastic individual with a rich life experience.

In addition to his work with the Bhagavad Gita, he is also an efficient Tarot card reader, Astro-Vastu consultant, and a talented singer and composer. He has sung the entire Ram Charita Manas and Bhagavad Gita in his own compositions, and has sung the phrase "Lokah Samastha Sukhino Bhavantu" in 50 different languages. He is currently working on a detailed and scientific study of Vedas, Upanishads, Puranas, and the Bhagavad Gita. He has also composed and sung the Hanuman Chalisa and Gayatri Mantra in 108 and 1008 different compositions, respectively.

Awards - Four Times Guinness World Records, Winner of Mahatma Gandhi Vishwa Shanti Puraskar, Mahatma Gandhi Global Peace Ambassador, Kashi Ratna Award, Dr. APJ Abdul Kalam Motivational Person of the Year 2017, Mother Teresa Award, Indira Gandhi Priyadarshini Award, Bharat Vikas Ratna Award, Udyog Ratna Award, Vigyan Prasar Award, Poorvanchal Ratn Samman.

Preface

The pursuit of happiness and fulfillment is a common goal for many people, but it is often the relationships that we have with others that make life truly rich and meaningful. The quality of our relationships has a profound impact on our well-being and can shape who we are as individuals. That's why it's so important to develop authentic relationships that are based on mutual respect, trust, and a shared sense of purpose.

In this book, "Secrets to Develop Authentic Relationships: Practical Strategies for Creating Lasting Connections," we will explore the key ingredients that are necessary for building meaningful and fulfilling relationships. Whether you are looking to deepen the connections you already have or seeking to establish new ones, the insights and strategies in this book will help you to create relationships that are based on mutual support, empathy, and a shared sense of purpose.

Through a combination of practical tips and exercises, we will cover a range of topics including building trust and communication, overcoming conflict and negativity, developing emotional intimacy, and much more. Whether you are in a romantic relationship, a friendship, a family relationship, or a professional partnership, the strategies outlined in this book can help you to create the meaningful and fulfilling relationships that you crave.

So, whether you are seeking to deepen your existing relationships, create new ones, or simply to become more effective in your interactions with others, this book offers a roadmap for achieving lasting connections and developing authentic relationships.

Prologue

Listen actively: One of the most important things you can do to support your partner is to listen to their goals and dreams. This means putting aside distractions and truly paying attention to what they have to say. Ask questions and show genuine interest in their aspirations.

Offer practical support: Depending on the nature of your partner's goals and dreams, you may be able to offer practical support that can help them get closer to achieving their objectives. This could include providing resources or introductions, or simply lending a hand to complete a project.

Encourage and motivate: Encouragement can be a powerful motivator. Offer your support and praise for your partner's efforts, and help them stay motivated by reminding them of their progress and why their goal is important to them.

Be a cheerleader: Celebrate your partner's successes and milestones, no matter how small they may seem. Show your excitement and support for their progress, and help them feel proud of their achievements.

Help them stay on track: Encourage your partner to set realistic, achievable goals and to break them down into smaller steps. Help them stay focused on their objectives, and offer support and advice when they face setbacks or challenges.

ONE

Discovering What Makes a Good Relationship

Building strong and authentic relationships is crucial for our overall happiness and well-being. In order to establish and maintain positive relationships, it's important to understand what makes a good relationship and what qualities to look for. This chapter will explore the essential elements of healthy relationships and provide practical tips for developing lasting connections.

Trust:

Trust is the foundation of any healthy relationship. It allows us to be vulnerable and open with each other, and fosters a sense of safety and security in the relationship. Without trust, it's difficult to build a strong, meaningful connection. To build trust, it's important to be honest and consistent in our actions and words, and to respect each other's boundaries.

Communication:

Effective communication is critical in any relationship. It allows us to understand each other's needs and perspectives, and helps us to resolve conflicts in a healthy and respectful way. Good communication involves active listening, expressing ourselves clearly and respectfully, and taking the time to understand each other's point of view.

Respect:

Mutual respect is another key component of a good relationship. This means treating each other with dignity and considering each other's feelings and needs. It also involves accepting each other's differences and valuing each other's opinions and beliefs.

Support:

Relationships thrive when both partners offer support and encouragement to each other. This can be in the form of emotional support, practical help, or simply being there for each other in good times and bad.

Common Interests:

Sharing common interests and hobbies can help to strengthen the bond between partners and bring joy to the relationship. Whether it's a shared passion for cooking, a love of hiking, or a shared appreciation for music, having common interests helps to keep the relationship fresh and exciting.

Flexibility:

Relationships are dynamic and can change over time, so it's important to be flexible and open to new experiences and perspectives. This can involve compromising, adapting to new challenges, and being willing to try new things together.

Intimacy:

Physical and emotional intimacy is an important aspect of a healthy relationship. It involves feeling close and connected to each other, and includes physical affection, such as hugging and kissing, as well as emotional intimacy, such as sharing thoughts and feelings.

In conclusion, good relationships are built on a foundation of trust, communication, respect, support, common interests, flexibility, and intimacy. By understanding these key elements and making an effort to cultivate them in our relationships, we can build strong, lasting connections and experience the joy and fulfillment that comes from authentic relationships.

"Real relationships are built on mutual trust and understanding, not just shared experiences."

♡♡♡

TWO

Building Trust and Communication

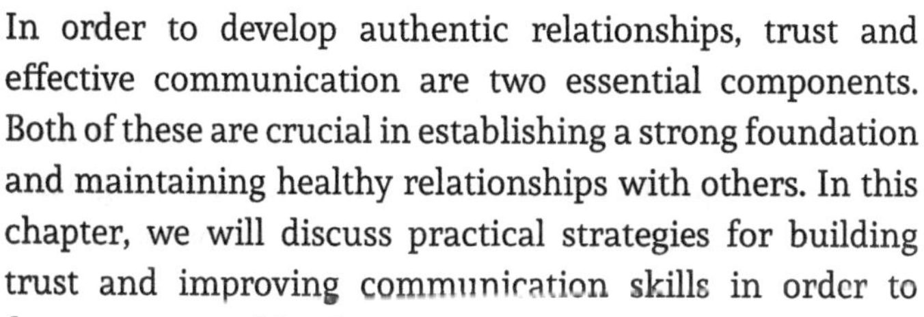

In order to develop authentic relationships, trust and effective communication are two essential components. Both of these are crucial in establishing a strong foundation and maintaining healthy relationships with others. In this chapter, we will discuss practical strategies for building trust and improving communication skills in order to foster strong and lasting connections.

Understanding the Importance of Trust

Trust is an essential component of all healthy relationships. It allows individuals to feel secure and confident in their interactions with others, knowing that they can rely on each other to be honest, reliable, and supportive. Without trust, it can be difficult to build meaningful connections and maintain healthy relationships over time.

Establishing Trust

Establishing trust in a relationship takes time, effort, and commitment from both parties. A few ways to build trust include being honest, following through on promises, being reliable, and being open and transparent with your feelings and intentions.

The Role of Communication

Effective communication is also key to building strong and authentic relationships. It allows individuals to understand each other's perspectives, express their feelings and needs, and resolve conflicts effectively.

Improving Communication Skills

Improving communication skills can be accomplished through various methods, including active listening, asking open-ended questions, avoiding criticism and judgment, and being open and non-defensive in your responses.

Communicating Difficult Feelings and Issues

It is important to address difficult feelings and issues in relationships, but it is also important to communicate these in a healthy and productive way. This can be achieved through active listening, empathy, and avoiding blame or criticism.

Building a Strong Foundation of Trust and Communication

By building trust and improving communication skills, individuals can establish a strong foundation for their relationships. This foundation allows for open and authentic communication, fosters intimacy, and lays the groundwork for lasting and meaningful connections.

In conclusion, building trust and communication are essential components of authentic relationships. By understanding the importance of these factors, individuals can take practical steps to improve their skills and foster strong and meaningful connections with others.

"Authentic relationships are not just about being there for each other in good times, but in bad times too."

THREE

Overcoming Conflict and Negativity

Conflict and negativity can arise in any relationship, whether it's with a romantic partner, family member, friend, or coworker. These challenges can test the strength of the relationship and, if not addressed properly, lead to a breakdown in communication and trust. However, with the right approach, conflict and negativity can be overcome, leading to a deeper, more authentic connection.

Here are some strategies for overcoming conflict and negativity in relationships:

Identify the root cause of the conflict.

Before you can find a solution to the conflict, you need to understand what is causing it. Take some time to reflect on your own feelings and motivations, and try to see the situation from the other person's point of view.

Practice active listening.

When in conflict, it's important to listen to the other person's perspective without interrupting or becoming defensive. Repeat back what you've heard to ensure you understand their point of view, and ask questions to clarify any misunderstandings.

Acknowledge feelings and validate emotions.

Conflict often arises from unmet emotional needs. When both parties feel heard and understood, it can help to ease tensions and create a more positive atmosphere for resolution.

Be open to compromise.

No one is always right or wrong in a conflict, so it's important to be open to finding a solution that works for both parties. This might mean making compromises or finding a middle ground.

Seek outside help.

If the conflict is particularly stubborn or complex, consider seeking the help of a mediator or counselor to facilitate communication and find a resolution.

Avoid blame and accusations.

Blaming and accusing the other person will only escalate

the conflict and make it more difficult to resolve. Instead, focus on finding a solution that works for both of you.

Use humor to diffuse tension.

Humor can be a powerful tool in resolving conflict, especially if both parties are willing to use it.

Take a break.

Sometimes, stepping away from a conflict for a little while can help both parties to calm down and gain some perspective.

Focus on the present and future, not the past.

The past is unchangeable, so it's important to focus on finding a solution for the present and future, rather than dwelling on what's already happened.

By following these strategies, you can overcome conflict and negativity in your relationships, leading to deeper, more authentic connections. With practice, these skills can become second nature, allowing you to create lasting, meaningful relationships with the people in your life.

"The foundation of a strong relationship is good communication and a willingness to listen."

FOUR

Cultivating Compassion and Empathy

In today's fast-paced world, it can be easy to become caught up in our own lives and lose sight of the struggles and challenges that others may be facing. However, developing compassion and empathy for others can be a powerful tool for building authentic relationships and creating lasting connections.

One of the key ways to cultivate compassion and empathy is through community service. Engaging in activities that help others can broaden your perspective and give you a deeper appreciation for the struggles and challenges others may face. Whether it's volunteering at a local soup kitchen, helping a neighbor in need, or participating in a charity event, these experiences can help you develop a sense of compassion and empathy for others.

Another way to cultivate compassion and empathy is by seeking to understand others' emotions. When interacting with others, it's important to pay attention to their body language, tone of voice, and other non-verbal cues. By doing so, you can gain a deeper understanding of what they may be feeling and respond with compassion.

It's also crucial to be kind and non-judgmental when engaging with others. Avoid making assumptions or passing judgment on others. Instead, strive to be understanding and compassionate. This mindset can help you form strong bonds and foster mutual understanding and respect.

Finally, practicing mindfulness can also help you cultivate compassion and empathy. Mindfulness helps you become more aware of your thoughts and emotions, as well as those of others. When you're mindful, you're better equipped to understand others and respond with compassion.

Follow the following also:

Participate in community service:

Engaging in activities that help others can be a great way to develop compassion and empathy. Whether it's volunteering at a local soup kitchen, helping a neighbor in need, or participating in a charity event, these experiences can help you see the world from a different perspective and develop a deeper appreciation for the challenges others may face.

Seek to understand others' emotions:

When interacting with others, pay attention to their body language, tone of voice, and other non-verbal cues. This can give you insight into their emotions and help you understand what they may be feeling.

Be kind and non-judgmental:

When engaging with others, it's important to be kind and non-judgmental. Avoid making assumptions or passing judgment on others. Instead, strive to be understanding and compassionate.

Practice mindfulness:

Mindfulness can help you become more aware of your thoughts and emotions, as well as those of others. When you're mindful, you're better equipped to understand others and respond with compassion.

By cultivating compassion and empathy, you can establish deeper, more meaningful connections with others and build relationships that are authentic and lasting. Whether it's in your personal life or in your professional life, these qualities can help you form strong bonds and foster mutual understanding and respect. So take some time to work on developing these skills, and you'll be well on your way to establishing lasting relationships and creating meaningful connections with others.

In conclusion, cultivating compassion and empathy is a key aspect of building authentic relationships and creating lasting connections. By working on developing these skills, you'll be well on your way to establishing meaningful connections with others, both in your personal and professional life.

"True intimacy comes from vulnerability, sharing your authentic self with another person."

FIVE

SUPPORTING EACH OTHER'S GOALS AND DREAMS

Building authentic relationships requires a strong foundation of mutual support and encouragement. When each person in a relationship feels that their partner is behind them, it can be a powerful motivator in achieving their individual goals and dreams. In this chapter, we will explore the key strategies for supporting each other's aspirations, and how to foster a relationship in which both individuals feel empowered to pursue their passions.

Listen actively:

One of the most important things you can do to support your partner is to listen to their goals and dreams. This means putting aside distractions and truly paying attention to what they have to say. Ask questions and show genuine interest in their aspirations.

Offer practical support:

Depending on the nature of your partner's goals and dreams, you may be able to offer practical support that can help them get closer to achieving their objectives. This could include providing resources or introductions, or simply lending a hand to complete a project.

Encourage and motivate:

Encouragement can be a powerful motivator. Offer your support and praise for your partner's efforts, and help them stay motivated by reminding them of their progress and why their goal is important to them.

Be a cheerleader:

Celebrate your partner's successes and milestones, no matter how small they may seem. Show your excitement and support for their progress, and help them feel proud of their achievements.

Help them stay on track:

Encourage your partner to set realistic, achievable goals and to break them down into smaller steps. Help them stay focused on their objectives, and offer support and advice when they face setbacks or challenges.

Avoid negative energy:

Avoid criticizing or downplaying your partner's goals and dreams. Instead, offer a positive, supportive environment that encourages them to keep going, even when things get tough.

Share your own aspirations:

Sharing your own goals and dreams can help your partner understand what you're going through, and provide them with a greater understanding of your perspective. Additionally, sharing your aspirations can help you both grow closer and strengthen your relationship.

By following these strategies, you can help create an environment in which both partners feel empowered to pursue their passions and achieve their dreams. A supportive relationship can be a powerful tool for personal growth and happiness, and by building a foundation of mutual support and encouragement, you can create a relationship that lasts a lifetime.

"Respect is the cornerstone of any successful relationship, it allows for growth and understanding."

SIX

Developing Emotional Intimacy

Emotional intimacy is a vital component of any authentic and lasting relationship. It refers to the level of trust and vulnerability that exists between two people, and is characterized by open and honest communication, empathy, and mutual support. Developing emotional intimacy involves taking the time to understand your own feelings and experiences, as well as those of your partner.

Here are some practical strategies for developing emotional intimacy in your relationships:

Practice active listening:

When your partner is talking to you, listen attentively and try to understand their perspective. Show that you care by asking questions and expressing empathy.

Share your thoughts and feelings:

Be open and honest about your thoughts, feelings, and experiences. Encourage your partner to do the same by creating a safe and non-judgmental space for them to share.

Show affection and physical intimacy:

Hugging, holding hands, and other forms of physical touch can help build emotional intimacy by creating a sense of closeness and connection.

Spend quality time together:

Spend time together doing activities that you both enjoy and that allow you to connect on an emotional level. This could be as simple as taking a walk or cooking a meal together.

Be present and engaged:

When you are with your partner, make sure to put away distractions and be fully present in the moment. This helps build emotional intimacy by showing that you value your relationship and your partner.

Practice empathy:

Try to understand your partner's perspective and feelings, even if they are different from your own. Empathy helps build emotional intimacy by creating a sense of understanding and support.

Seek outside help if needed:

If you are struggling to develop emotional intimacy, consider seeking the help of a therapist or counselor. They can provide you with tools and strategies for improving your relationship.

Developing emotional intimacy takes time and effort, but it is well worth it for the benefits it brings. When you have an emotionally intimate relationship, you feel supported, understood, and valued by your partner, which helps build trust, deepen your connection, and strengthen your bond.

"In a healthy relationship, both partners support each other's goals and dreams."

♡♡♡

SEVEN

Learning to Listen and Respect

Developing strong relationships requires active listening and showing respect to others. These skills are essential in creating a bond of trust and understanding that allows people to connect on a deeper level. By learning to listen, you become more attuned to the needs of others, and by showing respect, you demonstrate your willingness to accept and appreciate them for who they are.

Active listening involves more than simply hearing what someone has to say. It requires you to pay attention, ask questions, and show genuine interest in the other person. This type of listening helps you better understand their thoughts, feelings, and experiences, which in turn can help you build stronger connections with them.

Respect is another key component of building strong

relationships. It means recognizing and valuing the differences between people, and accepting that they have the right to their own opinions and beliefs. When you show respect, you create an atmosphere of trust and mutual understanding, which is essential for building lasting connections.

There are several ways to develop these skills. One effective method is to practice mindfulness and focus on being fully present in the moment. This can help you better understand the thoughts and feelings of others, and respond to them in a more meaningful way. Another way to build these skills is to engage in active listening exercises, such as taking turns sharing personal experiences and perspectives with a partner.

It is also important to understand that respect and active listening are not just about the words you say, but also about your body language and overall behavior. For example, making eye contact, nodding your head, and using an open and approachable posture can help demonstrate your respect and interest in the other person.

In conclusion, learning to listen and respect others is a key part of developing authentic relationships. By taking the time to actively listen and understand the perspectives and experiences of others, you can create a foundation of trust and understanding that will help you build lasting connections. Remember that building strong relationships takes time and effort, but the reward of having authentic and supportive relationships is worth it.

"The best relationships are those in which both partners continue to grow and evolve together."

♡♡♡

EIGHT

Accepting & Non-Judgmental

One of the key aspects of building authentic relationships is being accepting and non-judgmental. When you are able to let go of judgment and criticism, you create an environment of trust and respect. This opens up the possibility for deeper, more meaningful connections with the people in your life.

Acceptance is about acknowledging and embracing the differences in people, rather than trying to change them. This means that you are open to learning about others, their values, and what is important to them. When you are accepting, you create a safe space for others to be themselves, and they are more likely to trust you.

Non-judgmentalness is about letting go of the need to judge and evaluate others. Instead, you focus on understanding and empathy. When you approach others with a non-judgmental attitude, they are more likely to open up and share their thoughts and feelings with you.

To cultivate acceptance and non-judgmentalness, try the following:

Practice mindfulness:

Focus on being present in the moment and observing your thoughts and feelings without judgment.

Let go of your own biases:

Acknowledge that your own experiences and beliefs may not be the same as others. This can help you be more accepting of others.

Listen actively:

Practice active listening by focusing on what the other person is saying, rather than trying to anticipate what you want to say next.

Seek to understand:

Instead of trying to prove your point or win an argument, focus on understanding the other person's perspective.

Offer empathy:

Put yourself in the other person's shoes and try to understand what they are going through.

Ask questions:

Ask the other person about their experiences and perspectives, rather than assuming you know what they are thinking or feeling.

Let go of the need to control:

Accept that you cannot control other people's thoughts, feelings, or behavior.

By being accepting and non-judgmental, you create an environment of trust and respect that allows for deeper and more meaningful relationships. Remember that everyone has their own unique experiences and perspectives, and by embracing that, you can create strong and lasting connections with the people in your life.

"A relationship based on love, empathy, and compassion will last a lifetime."

NINE

Celebrating Each Other's Achievements

Relationships thrive when both partners support and celebrate each other's achievements. Celebrating each other's successes creates a positive and encouraging environment that strengthens the bond between partners.

In this chapter, we'll explore the importance of acknowledging and celebrating each other's achievements and how to do it in a meaningful way. We'll also examine some of the common obstacles that can prevent couples from celebrating each other's successes, and how to overcome them.

Why Celebrating Each Other's Achievements is Important

Celebrating each other's achievements helps to build mutual respect and appreciation. It shows that you value your partner's accomplishments and are invested in their growth and happiness. This type of positive reinforcement can boost your partner's confidence and help them feel more motivated to pursue their goals.

Additionally, celebrating each other's achievements can also help to reduce feelings of jealousy and competition that can sometimes arise in relationships. When partners are happy for each other's successes, it creates a supportive and positive environment where everyone can thrive.

How to Celebrate Each Other's Achievements

The key to celebrating each other's achievements is to make it personal and meaningful. Here are some suggestions:

Acknowledge their achievement: Start by simply acknowledging your partner's achievement and congratulating them. This can be as simple as saying "Congratulations! I'm so proud of you."

Share in the excitement: Show your excitement for their success by actively engaging in their celebration. Whether it's attending an awards ceremony, or simply joining in on a celebratory dinner, your participation will mean a lot to your partner.

Give a heartfelt gift: Give your partner a meaningful and personal gift to commemorate their achievement. This could be something as simple as a heartfelt note or a special piece of jewelry that symbolizes your love and support.

Show public support: Share your partner's achievement

with others by posting about it on social media or mentioning it to friends and family. This helps to acknowledge their success and spread positivity in your community.

Make it a special occasion: Turn your partner's achievement into a special occasion by planning a celebration. This could be anything from a romantic dinner to a weekend getaway, depending on what you both enjoy.

Overcoming Obstacles to Celebrating Each Other's Achievements

Although celebrating each other's achievements is important, there are sometimes obstacles that can get in the way. Here are some common challenges and ways to overcome them:

Jealousy: If you're feeling jealous of your partner's achievement, it's important to remember that their success is not a reflection of your own worth. Instead, focus on the positive aspects of their accomplishment and find ways to support and celebrate them.

Resentment: If you feel resentful about your partner's achievement, it may be because you feel like your own achievements are being overlooked. Take the time to talk to your partner about your feelings and work together to find ways to support each other's goals and dreams.

Competing interests: If you and your partner have competing interests, it can be difficult to celebrate each other's achievements. However, it's important to remember that you're a team and that celebrating each other's successes will only strengthen your relationship.

In conclusion, celebrating each other's achievements is an important aspect of any healthy and authentic relationship. By acknowledging and supporting each other's successes, you'll create a positive and encouraging environment where both partners can thrive.

"Conflict is inevitable in relationships, but it's how we handle it that determines its outcome."

TEN

Listening without Interrupting

Listening without interrupting is an essential aspect of building authentic relationships. In many cases, people feel that they have to constantly interrupt others in order to make their point heard or to show that they are engaged in the conversation. However, this behavior can be perceived as dismissive or disrespectful. It's important to understand that the act of listening is just as important as speaking in any relationship.

Here are some key strategies for practicing effective listening without interrupting:

Pay Attention: When someone is speaking, give them your full attention. Avoid distractions such as your phone, computer, or other people.

Avoid Jumping to Conclusions: Don't assume you know what the person is going to say before they finish speaking. Listen with an open mind, and wait until they have finished before responding.

Practice Active Listening: Show the person that you are listening by making eye contact, nodding, and using non-verbal cues such as gestures. This helps demonstrate that you are engaged in the conversation.

Take Notes: If you need to remember something that the person is saying, take notes. This helps you stay focused on the conversation and allows you to reflect on what the person is saying after the conversation is over.

Ask Questions: If you're not sure about something the person is saying, ask questions. This shows that you're interested in the conversation and helps to clarify any misunderstandings.

Avoid Interrupting: Don't interrupt the person when they are speaking. Wait until they have finished before responding. If you're not sure if you understood what the person was saying, ask them to repeat it.

Show Empathy: Try to put yourself in the other person's shoes and understand their perspective. This helps you connect with the person on a deeper level and shows that you care about their feelings.

Incorporating these strategies into your daily life can greatly improve your ability to listen without interrupting and build stronger, more authentic relationships. By making a conscious effort to listen and understand others, you can demonstrate your respect and appreciation for their thoughts and ideas. Ultimately, this will help you to build stronger, more meaningful connections with others.

"The key to a lasting connection is finding common ground and shared values."

ELEVEN

Resolving Problems with Respect

In any relationship, conflicts and problems are bound to arise. However, the way these issues are addressed can either strengthen or weaken the bond between individuals. It's essential to approach problems with respect and a willingness to find a mutually beneficial solution.

Here are some strategies for resolving problems in a respectful and healthy manner:

Listen actively:

When resolving problems, it's crucial to listen to the other person's point of view. Try to understand their perspective and acknowledge their feelings. Avoid interrupting and be open to hearing their side of the story.

Communicate openly:

Express your own feelings and opinions in a clear and respectful manner. Share your thoughts and feelings without attacking or blaming the other person.

Focus on the issue:

Stay focused on the problem at hand and avoid bringing up past issues or unrelated matters. Try to keep the conversation solution-oriented and focused on finding a mutually agreeable solution.

Avoid assumptions:

Don't assume that you know what the other person is thinking or feeling. Ask questions and clarify any misunderstandings.

Take a break:

If the conversation is getting heated or emotionally charged, take a break to cool down. Return to the discussion when both parties are calm and ready to find a solution.

Compromise:

Be open to finding a middle ground and compromising. A solution that works for both parties is more likely to be successful in the long run.

Be accountable:

Take responsibility for your actions and be willing to make changes if necessary. Be open to feedback and willing to work together to improve the relationship.

By approaching problems with respect and a willingness to find a solution, individuals can strengthen their bond and build a lasting, authentic relationship. Remember, communication is key and both parties should be willing to listen and work together to resolve conflicts.

"By embracing each other's differences, we strengthen our relationships and grow together."

♡♡♡

TWELVE

DEVELOPING A SHARED VISION

When two people are in a relationship, it is essential that they share a common goal or vision for the future. Having a shared vision helps to create a sense of purpose and direction, which can lead to increased happiness and fulfillment. Moreover, it promotes a feeling of unity and ensures that both partners are working towards the same goals.

Here are some steps to help you and your partner develop a shared vision:

Communicate openly:

The first step towards developing a shared vision is open and honest communication. It is essential that both partners express their thoughts, feelings, and aspirations clearly and without any hesitation. This helps to establish a strong foundation for the relationship and builds trust.

Identify common interests:

Identifying common interests is a crucial step in developing a shared vision. Both partners should take the time to reflect on their individual goals and aspirations, as well as their shared interests. This can help to identify areas of commonality and establish a shared direction for the future.

Encourage creativity:

When developing a shared vision, it is important to be creative and open to new ideas. Encourage each other to dream big and think outside the box. This helps to broaden your perspectives and create a more comprehensive and diverse vision.

Create a shared goal:

Once you have identified your shared interests and aspirations, it's time to create a shared goal. This goal should reflect the unique aspirations and interests of both partners, while also incorporating a shared vision for the future.

Action plan:

With a shared goal in place, it's time to create an action plan. This plan should outline the steps necessary to achieve your shared vision, and assign specific tasks to each partner. It is important to be realistic about what you can achieve, but also to push yourself to grow and develop as a team.

Celebrate milestones:

As you work towards your shared vision, it's important to celebrate milestones along the way. This helps to keep you motivated and reinforces the importance of your shared vision.

Developing a shared vision is an ongoing process that requires patience, dedication, and open communication. However, the benefits of having a shared vision are immense, and can help to create a more meaningful and fulfilling relationship. Whether it's a shared dream for the future, a shared passion for a particular cause, or simply a shared sense of purpose, a shared vision can help to bring you and your partner closer together and create a more authentic and lasting connection.

"Building a positive atmosphere in our relationships fosters love and growth."

♡♡♡

THIRTEEN

Determining Internal Values and Beliefs

In order to build and maintain strong, authentic relationships, it is important to understand and embrace your own internal values and beliefs. Your values and beliefs shape your behavior, attitudes, and perspective, and they play a crucial role in the way you interact with others. By understanding your own values and beliefs, you can use this knowledge to form deeper connections and build more meaningful relationships.

To start, consider what is truly important to you. What do you believe in, and what values do you hold dear? For example, some people may place a high value on honesty, while others may prioritize their spiritual beliefs. There are no right or wrong answers; what is important is that you are aware of your own values and beliefs.

Once you have a clear understanding of your own values and beliefs, it is important to be open and honest about them with your loved ones. Open communication about your values and beliefs can help build trust and create a foundation for a healthy relationship. When both partners have a clear understanding of each other's values and beliefs, it is easier to avoid conflicts and find common ground.

In a relationship, it is natural for partners to have differing values and beliefs. It is important to respect each other's unique perspectives and work together to find common ground. When both partners are open and honest about their values and beliefs, they are more likely to support and encourage each other, even in the face of differences.

At the same time, it is also important to be mindful of your own biases and to avoid imposing your values and beliefs on others. Instead, approach your relationships with an open mind and a willingness to listen and learn from others.

In conclusion, determining and understanding your own values and beliefs is a crucial step in building strong, authentic relationships. By embracing your own values and beliefs, and being open and respectful with your loved ones, you can create a strong foundation for lasting connections.

"In authentic relationships, both partners listen to each other, respect each other, and support each other."

♡♡♡

FOURTEEN

Going on Meaningful Adventures Together

Creating lasting relationships involves sharing experiences and exploring the world together. Going on adventures, big or small, can help strengthen your connection, bring you closer, and foster trust. Whether it's trying a new hobby, taking a trip, or exploring your city, having shared experiences helps you grow together and create memories that will last a lifetime.

Here are some tips for going on meaningful adventures together:

Make it a priority:

Scheduling time for adventures should be an important

part of your routine. Whether it's once a month or once a year, make sure to set aside time to explore and have fun together.

Choose activities that interest both of you:

Select adventures that both partners will enjoy. This way, you can both be fully invested in the experience and have a better time.

Set realistic expectations:

It's important to be mindful of what each person is comfortable with and what the goal of the adventure is. Make sure you are both on the same page and know what to expect.

Open up to new experiences:

Be willing to step out of your comfort zone and try something new. Sometimes the best adventures come from trying something you wouldn't normally do.

Be flexible:

Be open to changing plans if necessary and don't get too attached to a specific outcome. The most important thing is to enjoy each other's company.

Have fun:

Don't take everything too seriously and remember to have fun. Adventures are a time to relax and let go of stress.

Take time to reflect:

After each adventure, take some time to reflect on the experience. Share your thoughts and feelings with each other and talk about what you learned and how you can apply it to your relationship.

Going on adventures together can be a fun and meaningful way to strengthen your relationship and create lasting memories. By being open to new experiences, flexible, and having fun, you can develop a deeper connection and build a foundation for a long-lasting relationship.

"Going on meaningful adventures together helps build a bond and strengthens relationships."

♡♡♡

FIFTEEN

Creating a Positive Atmosphere for Growth and Love

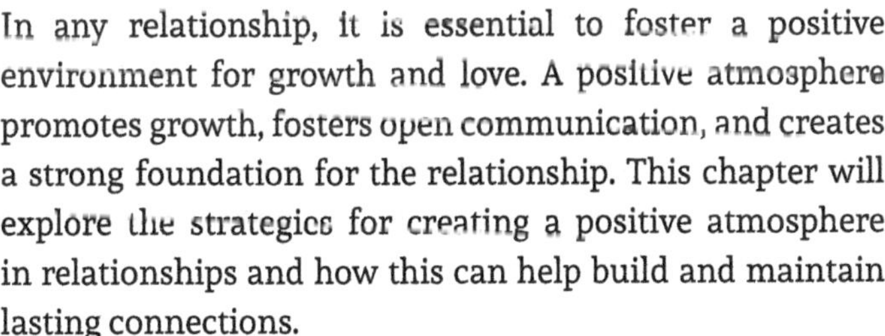

In any relationship, it is essential to foster a positive environment for growth and love. A positive atmosphere promotes growth, fosters open communication, and creates a strong foundation for the relationship. This chapter will explore the strategies for creating a positive atmosphere in relationships and how this can help build and maintain lasting connections.

Establish a Shared Sense of Purpose: A shared sense of purpose is the foundation of any strong relationship. When partners have a shared goal or vision, they work together to achieve it, which strengthens the bond between them. In relationships, having a shared purpose can be as simple as wanting to support each other in personal or professional growth, or as complex as building a life together.

Foster Open Communication: Open communication is essential for creating a positive atmosphere in relationships. It allows partners to express their feelings, thoughts, and ideas in a supportive environment, which helps to build trust and intimacy. Encourage your partner to be open and honest with you, and respond to their thoughts and feelings with empathy and understanding.

Encourage Personal Growth: Personal growth is essential for both partners in a relationship. Encouraging each other to grow and reach their full potential helps to build self-esteem and create a positive atmosphere for growth and love. Encouragement can be expressed through words of affirmation, providing opportunities for personal growth, or by simply listening and being supportive.

Practice Gratitude: Gratitude helps to foster a positive atmosphere in relationships by focusing on the good things in life. Expressing gratitude towards each other helps to strengthen the bond between partners and promote a sense of appreciation for each other. Start a gratitude jar or write letters of gratitude to each other regularly to cultivate a positive atmosphere.

Celebrate Each Other's Successes: Celebrating each other's successes helps to build a positive atmosphere in relationships. It promotes a sense of pride and respect for each other and strengthens the bond between partners.

Take the time to acknowledge and celebrate each other's achievements, no matter how big or small they may be.

Encourage Playfulness and Laughter: Playfulness and laughter are essential for creating a positive atmosphere in relationships. Laughter is a powerful tool for relieving stress, improving mood, and building a sense of intimacy. Encourage playfulness and laughter in your relationship by doing fun activities together, playing games, or simply being silly with each other.

Be Forgiving: Forgiveness is essential for creating a positive atmosphere in relationships. Holding grudges and resentment can create negativity and damage the relationship, but forgiving your partner can help to heal and move forward. Practice forgiveness regularly to maintain a positive atmosphere and a strong connection with your partner.

In conclusion, creating a positive atmosphere in relationships is essential for building and maintaining lasting connections. By focusing on open communication, personal growth, gratitude, celebration, playfulness, forgiveness, and more, you can foster an environment of love and growth in your relationship. By implementing these strategies, you will build a strong foundation for a happy and fulfilling relationship.

"True love is not about being perfect, it's about accepting each other's imperfections and choosing to grow together."

Other Books Of The Author

1. The Moments When I Met God
2. Kashiyile Theertha Pathangal
3. GURU GYAN VANI
4. Abhiprerak Gita
5. ASSI SE JAIN GHAT TAK
6. Hopelessness of Arjuna
7. The Soul and It's True Nature
8. Sense of Action (Karma)
9. Action through Wisdom
10. Action through Wisdom
11. THEORY AND PRACTICAL OF EVERY ACTION
12. LOGICAL UNDERSTANDING OF THE SUPREME
13. THE IMPERISHABLE SUPREME
14. Yatra Nishadraj se Hanuman Ghat Tak
15. Yatra Karnatak Ghat se Raja Ghat Tak
16. Yatra Pandey Ghat se Prayagraj Ghat Tak
17. Yatra Ranjendra Prasad Ghat se Dattatreya Ghat Tak
18. YaatraSindhiya Ghat se Gwaliar Ghat Tak
19. Yatra Mangala Gauri Ghat se Hanuman Gadhi Ghat Tak
20. Yatra Gaay Ghat Se Nishad Ghat Tak
21. MAA GANGA, GHATEN EVM UTSAV
22. Ganga Arti Dev Deepavali evam Any Utsav
23. Potentials of Digitalized India
24. VEDIC CONSCIOUSNESS
25. A Brief Introduction to Vedic Science
26. Kashi ke Barah Jyotirling
27. IMPACT OF MOTIVATION
28. Let's have a Milky Way Journey
29. Color Therapy in a Nutshell

30. Rigveda in a Nutshell
31. Yajurveda in a Nutshell
32. Samveda in a Nutshell
33. Atharva Veda in a Nutshell
34. Ayushman Bhava - Ayurveda
35. Srimad Bhagavad Gita and Upanishad Connection
36. Srimad Bhagavad Gita - an attempt to summarize each chapter.
37. Facts and Impact of Nakshatra
38. Astro Gems - NAVARATNA
39. Ekadashi - A Concise Overview
40. A Concise View of Hanuman Chalisa
41. Inspirational Gita
42. Nakshatraranyam
43. Summary of 18 Mahapuranas
44. Synopsis of 18 Upa Puranas
45. Rigvediya Upanishads
46. Shukla Yajurvediya Upanishads
47. Krishna Yajurvediya Upanishads
48. Samavediya Upanishads
49. Atharvavediya Upanishads
50. The Seven Great Sages
51. From Rocket Scientist to President Dr. APJ Abdul Kalam
52. The Visionary's Voice - Quotes of Dr. APJ Abdul Kalam
53. The Wisdom of Swami Vivekananda: Insights and Inspiration from a Legendary Spiritual Teacher
54. Ayurvedic Remedies from the Garden
55. Sages and Seers
56. Rising Strong – Motivational Stories of Women
57. Beyond Flames -Mystery stories of Funeral Ghat Manikarnika
58. The Origins of Tulsi: A Look at the Mythological Roots of the Plant"

59. The Holistic Cow: A Look at the Physical, Spiritual, and Cultural Importance of Cows in India
60. Arts of Healing
61. Exploring the Divine
62. Understanding Five Elements
63. The Etymology of Ram
64. Symbols of India
65. Voice of Change (About Speeches of Great Men)
66. She Speaks (About Speeches of Great Women)
67. Patriotism on Celluloid – Brief About Patriotic Films
68. The Music of Motivation: A Brief Guide to Inspirational Film Songs
69. **Unlocking the Secrets of the Dashopanishads**
70. A Cultural Mosaic
71. Ancient Traditions, Modern Minds
72. Ecos of Ancient Wisdom
73. Beneath the Surface
74. From Temples to Ashrams
75. Sages of the Subcontinent
76. The Art of Healling (Ayurveda, Yoga & Naturopathy)
77. Indian Kitchen
78. The Festivals of India
79. The Indian Epics Retold
80. The Power of Mantras
81. The Indian River Ganges
82. The Indian Architecture
83. Rites of Passage
84. The Indian Silk Road
85. The Indian Literature
86. The Indian Villages
87. The Indian Folks & Crafts
88. The Way of Buddha
89. The Ramayan of Tulsidas

90. Astrological Remedies
91. The Secret Power of Motivation
92. Secret of Developing your Inner Strength
93. The Secret Path to Motivation
94. The Art and Secret of Positive Thinking
95. The Secrets of Practicing Ethical Living
96. Indian Art and Painting
97. The Indian Herbalism
98. Bharatanatyam to Kathak
99. Exploring India's Astrological Remedies
100. The Indian Festival of Flowers
101. Indian Handicrafts
102. The Splashes of Joy – India's Colour Festival
103. The Indian Science of Astrology
104. The Indian Mythology
105. Path to Enlightenment
106. The Indian Spirituality for Children
107. Aromas of India
108. The Secrets of Healthy Relationships
109. Ancestral Ties
110. The Indian Street Food
111. Discovering America
112. The Indian Textile
113. Listening to Motivational Speeches
114. Taste of India
115. A Cultural Journey through Indian Nuptials
116. Motivational Quote for Change
117. Secret Strategies for Making Money
118. Secrets to Cultivate a Positive Mindset
119. A Tapestry of Cultures: Exploring India from Kashmir to Kanyakumari
120. Achieving Your Dreams with Resilience: Secret Strategies for Overcoming Obstacles

121. Innovative Startups - 25 Startup Ideas to Spark Your Business Creativity
122. Export Management: Strategies for Global Success
123. Exporting from India - A Step by Step Guide
124. Finance Fundamentals: Mastering Financial Management for Business Success
125. Global Growth Strategies for International Business Development
126. Marketing Mastery: Unlocking the Secrets of Modern Marketing
127. Operations Mastery: Managing the Flow of Value in Business
128. Strategic Business Management: Navigating the Modern Business Landscape
129. Human Resource Management Strategies for Building and Managing a High Performance Team
130. The Indian Landscapes and Nature: An Exploration Of India's Natural Beauty And Diversity
131. The Indian Street Performances: A Cultural Exploration of India's Street Performances
132. Affirming Your Self-Worth: Strategies for Achieving Emotional Wellbeing
133. Cultivating Self-Discipline: Secrets Methods for Achieving Your Goals
134. Embracing Change: Strategies for Adapting to Life's Challenges
135. Embracing Your Uniqueness: Secret Strategies for Living an Authentic Life
136. Finding Motivation in Despondency: Coping with Difficult Times
137. Embracing Change
138. Learning to Love Yourself
139. Managing Time for Yourself

140. Unlock the keys to Self-Motivation
141. Secret to Boost Confidence
142. Unlocking your Potential: A Path to Innerstrengh & Success
143. Secrets to Develop Authentic Relationship

Contact

DR. JAGADEESH PILLAI

MBA & PhD in Vedic Science

Four Times Guinness World Record Holder

Winner of Mahatma Gandhi Vishwa Shanti Puraskar and Global Peace Ambassador

Gemology, Astro & Vastu Consultant - Spiritual Counselor

Consultant for designing World Record Ideas

Efficient Tarot Card Reader

9839093003

myrichindia@gmail.com

drjagadeeshpillai@facebook

drjagadeeshpillai@instagram
jagadeeshpillai@youtube

www. JAGADEESHPILLAI.com

|| LOKAHA SAMASTHAHA SUKHINO BHAVANTU ||

9 798889 593218

Printed by Libri Plureos GmbH in Hamburg,
Germany